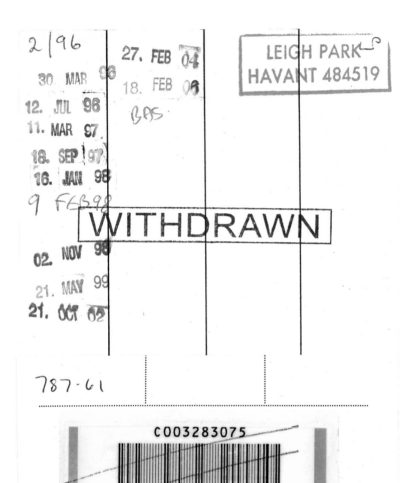

GUITAR STYLES!

Bass

SEA

ALPHONSO JOHNSON

COMPILED AND EDITED BY MICHAEL STIMPSON

CONTENTS

Solo

Reggae 1   4

Malcolm's Blues   6

Montuno   8

Reggae 2   10

Funk   12

Hip Hop   14

Brazilia   16

Alphonso's Bop   18

Waltz for Ana Maria   20

Cee Jay   22

Something About August   24

Bop 'Til you Drop   26

Aquarius   28

Duo

Rock Duo 1   30

Rock Duo 2   33

Rock Duo 3   36

The Elusive Lion   39

Trio

Secret Sisters   43

General Information   46

Music Department
OXFORD UNIVERSITY PRESS
Oxford and New York

Oxford University Press, Walton Street, Oxford OX2 6DP
© Oxford University Press 1994
Photocopying this copyright material is ILLEGAL

Designed by Paul Cleal
Cover designed by Rowie Christopher
Music engraved by Barnes Music Engraving Ltd.
Printed in Great Britain by Caligraving Ltd.

WELCOME TO GUITAR STYLES!

Guitar Styles! is a new concept in guitar publishing—it gives you the chance to stretch your skills and learn Bass, Classical, Flamenco, Folk, Jazz, and Rock styles, using your own instrument.

There are hints from each composer on how to achieve the authentic sound of each style.

Whether you're a beginner or more experienced guitarist, a teacher or student, this is the series for you to try some new solos and to play the ensemble pieces with your friends.

Why not try *Guitar Styles! Rock* next?

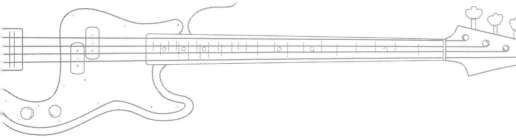

Reggae 1

This bass line is a very lively, rhythmic approach to playing the reggae style. Most reggae bass lines have a heavy, crotchet (quarter note) feel, so this semi-quaver (sixteenth note) emphasis gives a more snappy effect.

Rhythm for chords

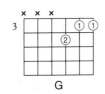
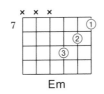
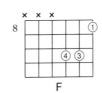
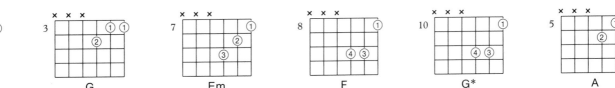
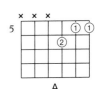

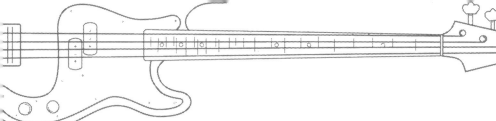

Malcolm's Blues

This piece should help you to realize the importance of keeping good time. It is a slow blues which uses a chromatic scale to link the chords.

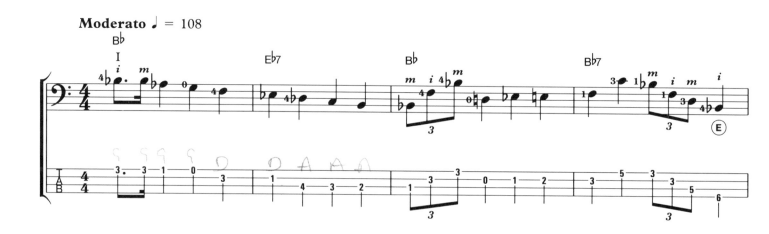

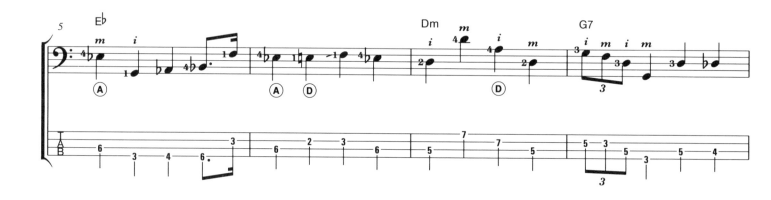

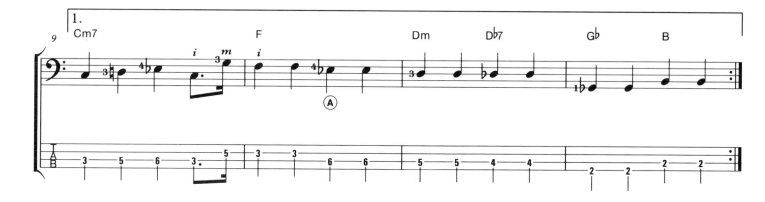

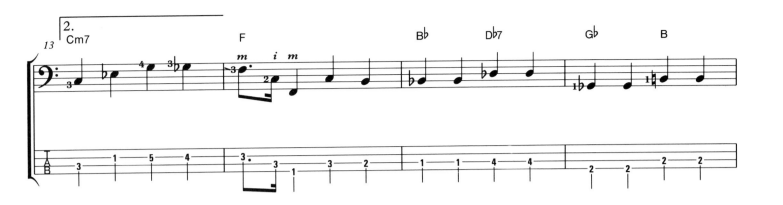

Rhythm for chords

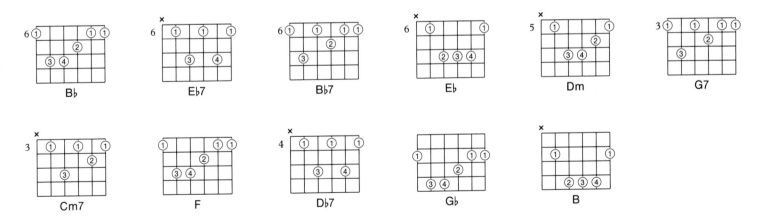

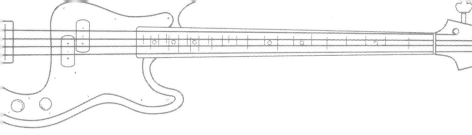

Montuno

This is a typical bass line in the Montuno style, which almost always contains a tied note or rest on the down beat of the third beat. It is important to relax when playing this style. All the notes and rests should receive their full value and not be rushed.

Andante ♩ = 88

Rhythm for chords

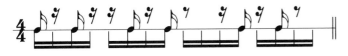

 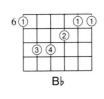 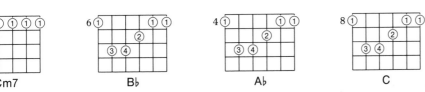

| Cm7 | Bb | Ab | C |

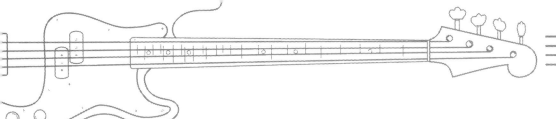

Reggae 2

This bass line should have a very laid-back feeling and be played legato (smoothly) to allow you to play a melodic and rhythmic bass part which features the bass in its dual role.

Rhythm for chords

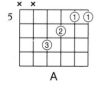
A

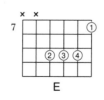
E

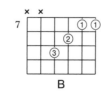
B

D

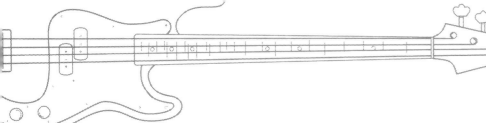

Funk

Interpretation is important for making the execution of the bass line work. Pay close attention to the accents, and try to make it fun to play even though it has a serious sound.

Rhythm for chords

Bars 9–12

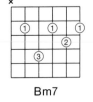 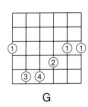 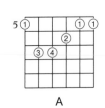 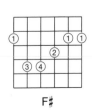 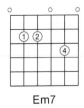

Bm7   G   A   F#   Em7

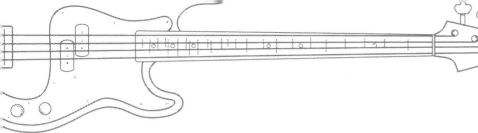

Hip Hop

This piece should have the swing-feel of jazz music combined with the rhythmic strength of rock.

Rhythm for chords

Bars 5–6, 11–12, 15

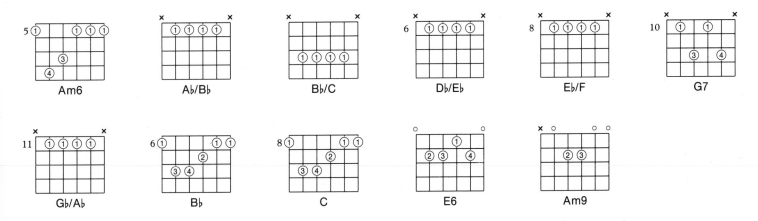

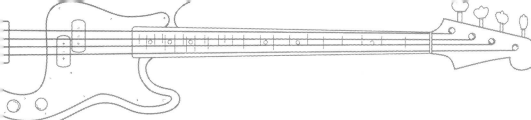

Brazilia

This samba bass line is also very melodic in the way it connects the chords. It should have a lively feeling, and be played as if it were a bass solo.

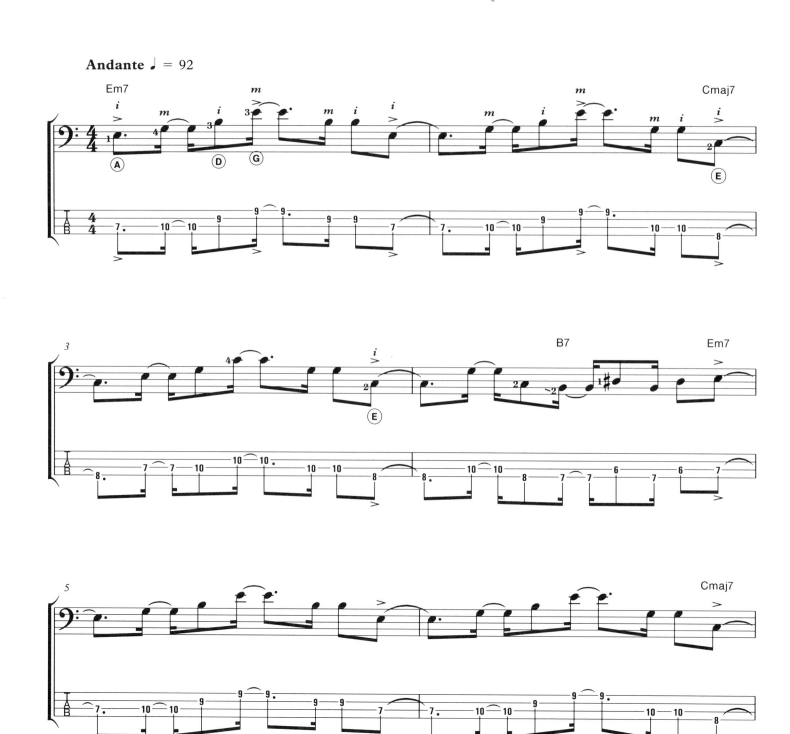

Rhythm for chords

Bar 10

Em7

Cmaj7

B7

F#dim7

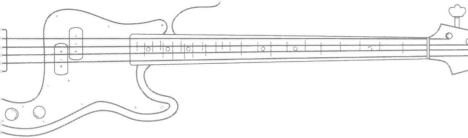

Alphonso's Bop

I have provided some alternative chord changes to a 12-bar blues so that other passing tones are available in this fast tempo walking bass line. The piece is written for a five-string bass and has a low Eb. If playing it on a four-string bass either take the note up an octave or re-tune the E string before beginning the piece.

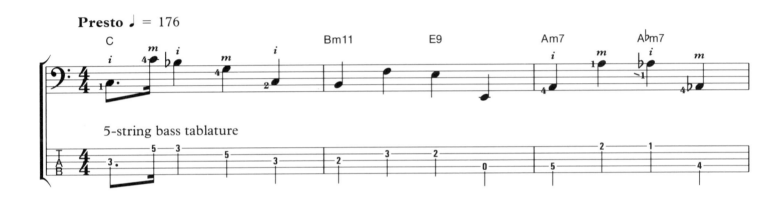

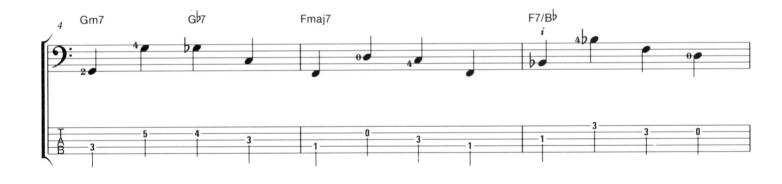

* If playing on a 4-string bass, play this note an octave higher.

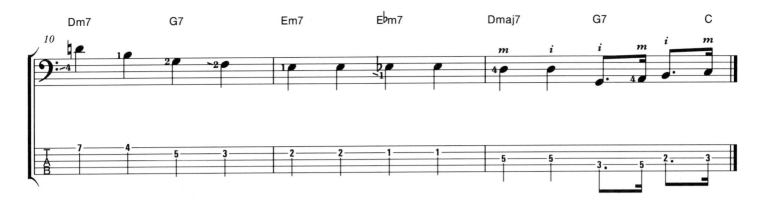

Rhythm for chords

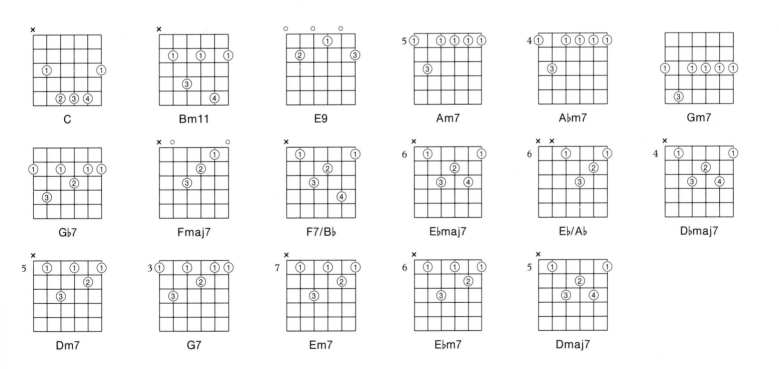

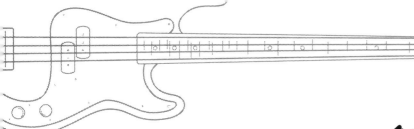

Waltz for Ana Maria

This piece will sound particularly expressive if you have a fretless bass.

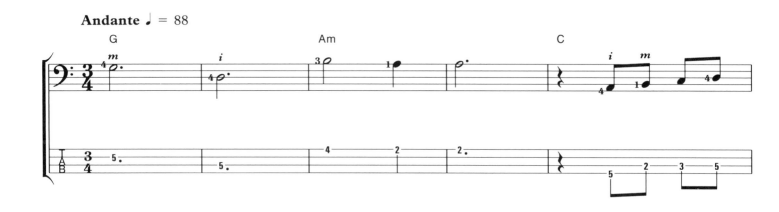

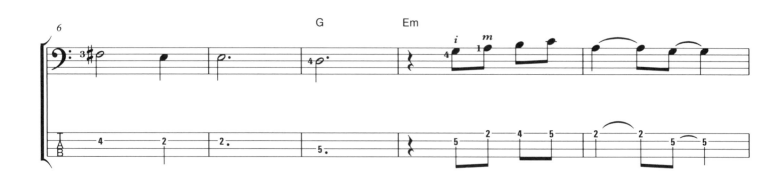

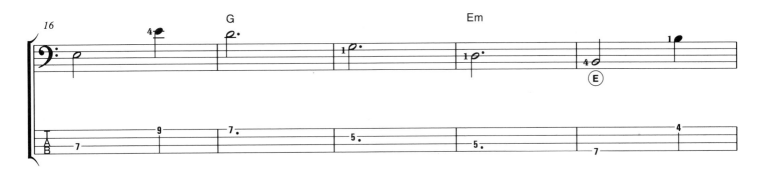

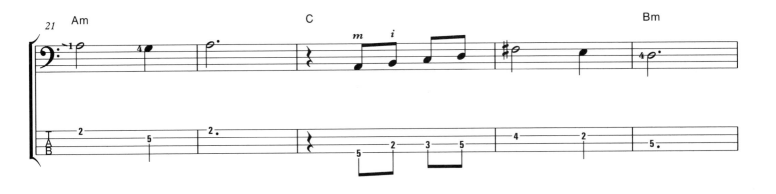

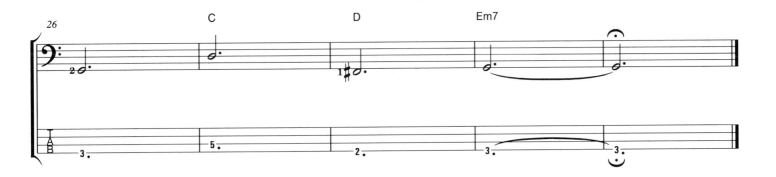

Rhythm for chords

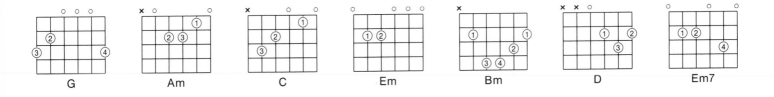

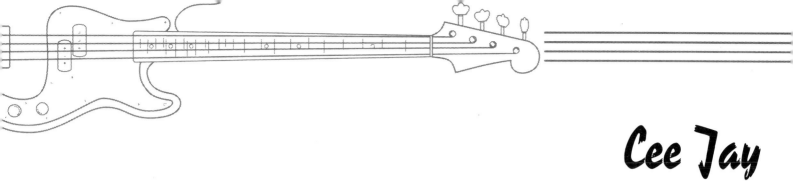

Cee Jay

Like 'Waltz for Ana Maria', this piece is especially suited to the sound of a fretless bass.

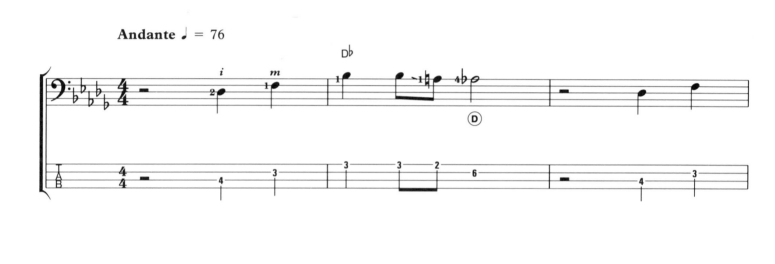

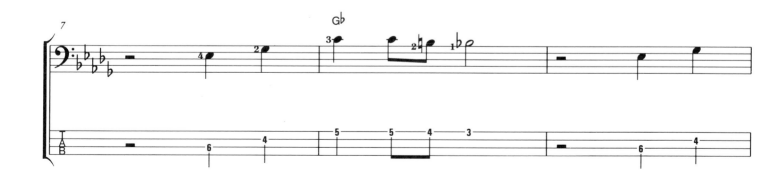

Rhythm for chords

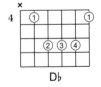

Db

Gb

Fm7

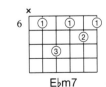

Ebm7

Abm

Bbm7

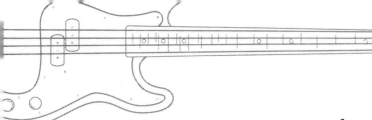

Something about August

This is a melody that requires two notes played together, as well as single notes. Try to play the melody imagining that the bass is like a saxophone. The piece is for a five-string bass and has a low E♭. If playing it on a four-string bass play the marked notes (*) up an octave.

Allegro ♩ = 160

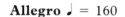

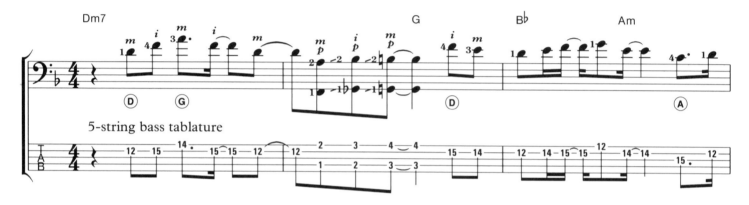

5-string bass tablature

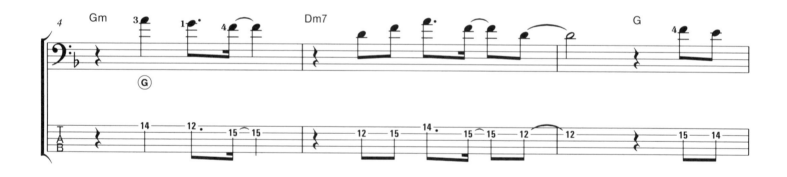

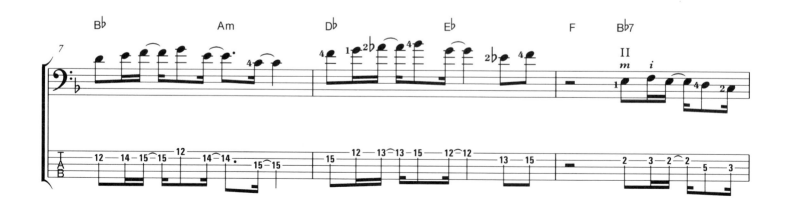

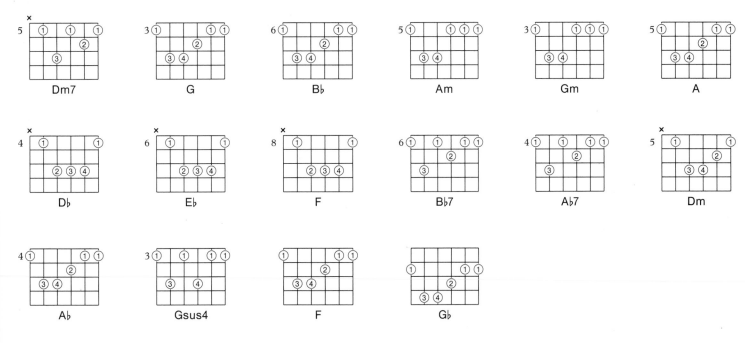

* If playing on 4-string bass play both notes an octave higher.

Rhythm – the chords should support the bass melody.

Bop 'Til you Drop

This melody is really two bass parts, because it has a tune on top of a continuing rhythm.
Try to play the melody a little louder than the rhythm line.

Allegro ♩ = 168

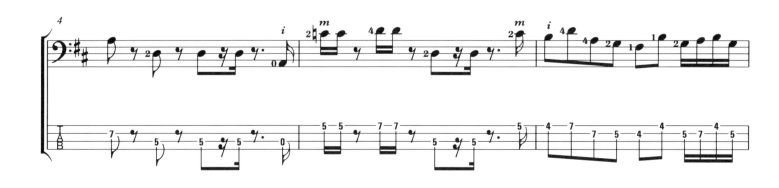

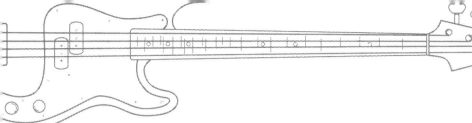

Aquarius

This melody was written for the fretless bass. If you're playing on a fretted bass, try it up an octave.

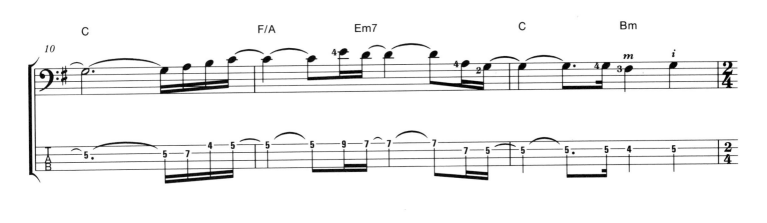

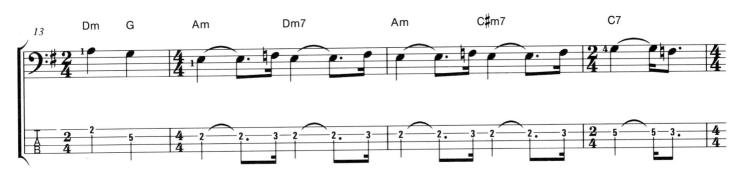

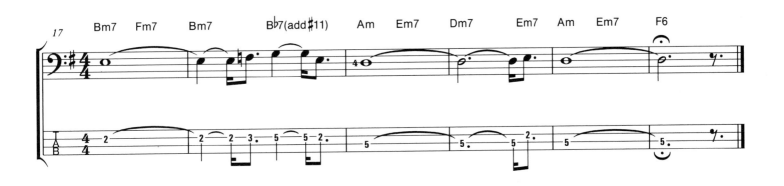

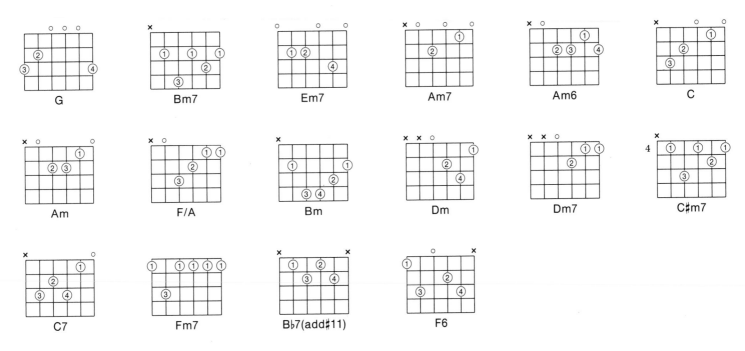

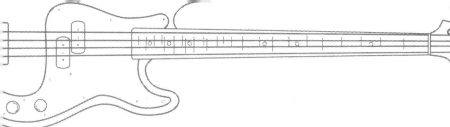

Rock Duo 1

This bass line sounds good when played with a combination of slapping (with the thumb) on the quavers (eighth notes) and plucking (with a finger) at the semi-quavers (sixteenth notes). The attitude should be mean-spirited but still with a sense of not taking it too seriously.

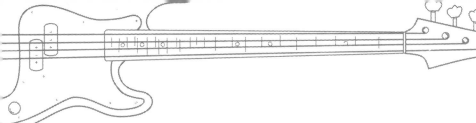

Rock Duo 2

Using the thumb to slap the notes that are slurred gives the right feel to this piece.

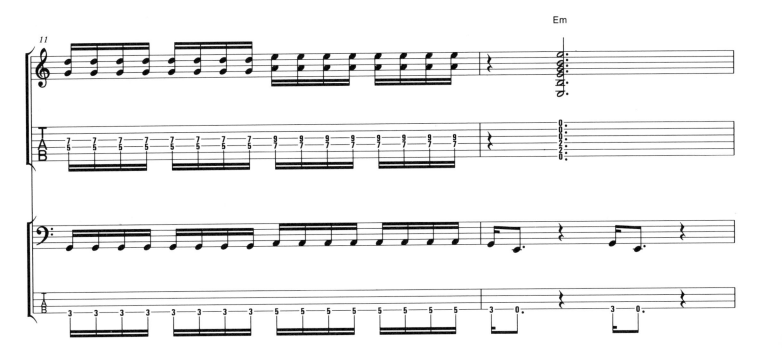

Em   Am

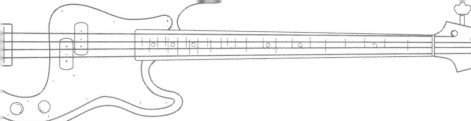

Rock Duo 3

This rhythmic and energetic bass line requires some efficient work by the plucking fingers. Every now and then the rhythm guitar should leave the chords and mimic the bass melody. Keep the line tight by damping the chords and observing the rests.

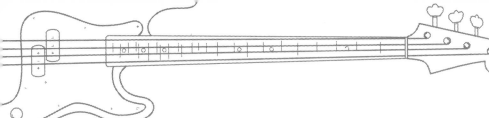

The Elusive Lion

As this piece is a very rhythmic Latin composition, it allows the bassist to play in different time signatures. A five-string bass should be used in order to achieve the lower notes, although a four-string bass with the E-string tuned down to D can be used.

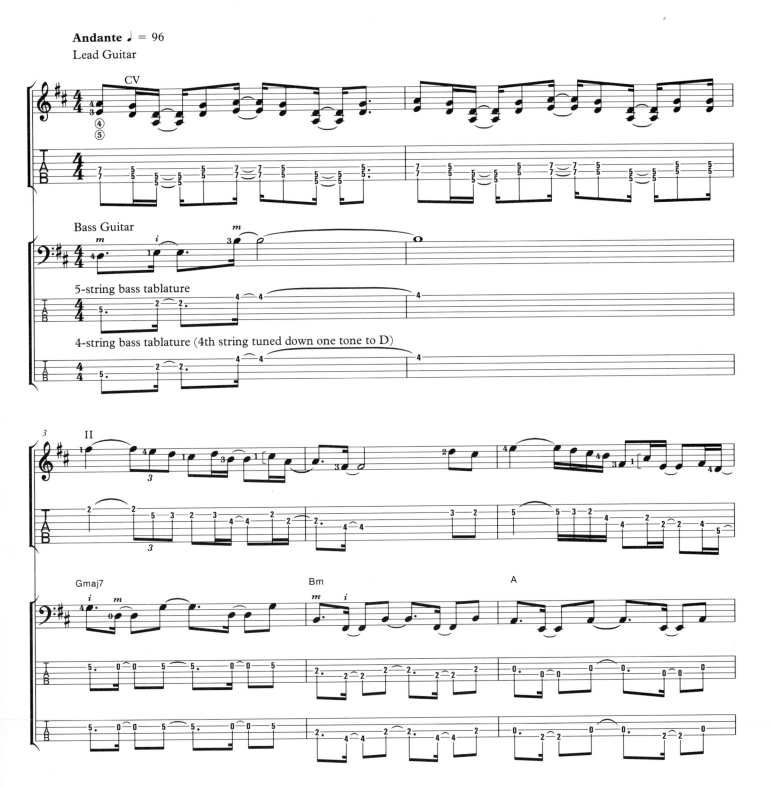

39

Rhythm for chords

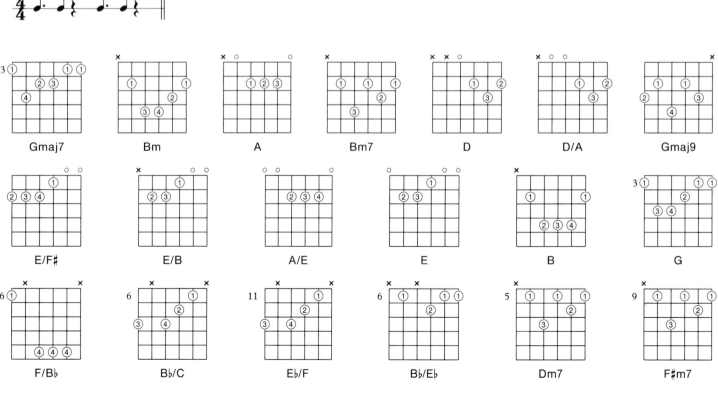

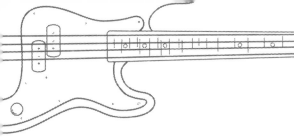

Secret Sisters

The bass melody should be played as if it were improvised, before beginning a walking bass line derived from the chord changes. This piece requires the bassist to switch from being the soloist to taking a more supportive role.

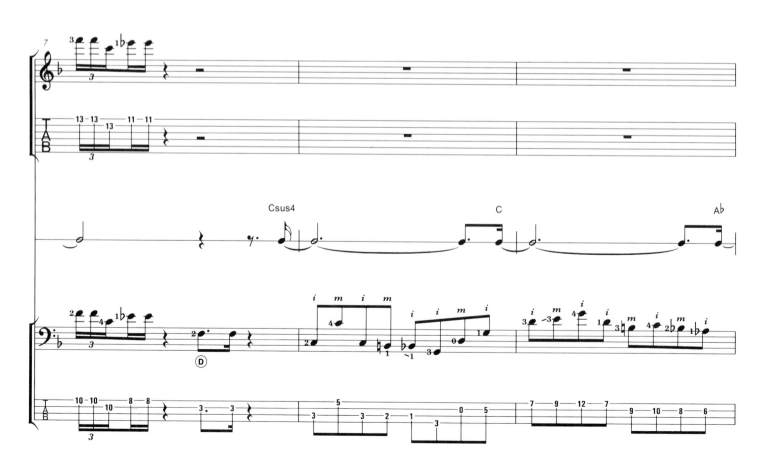

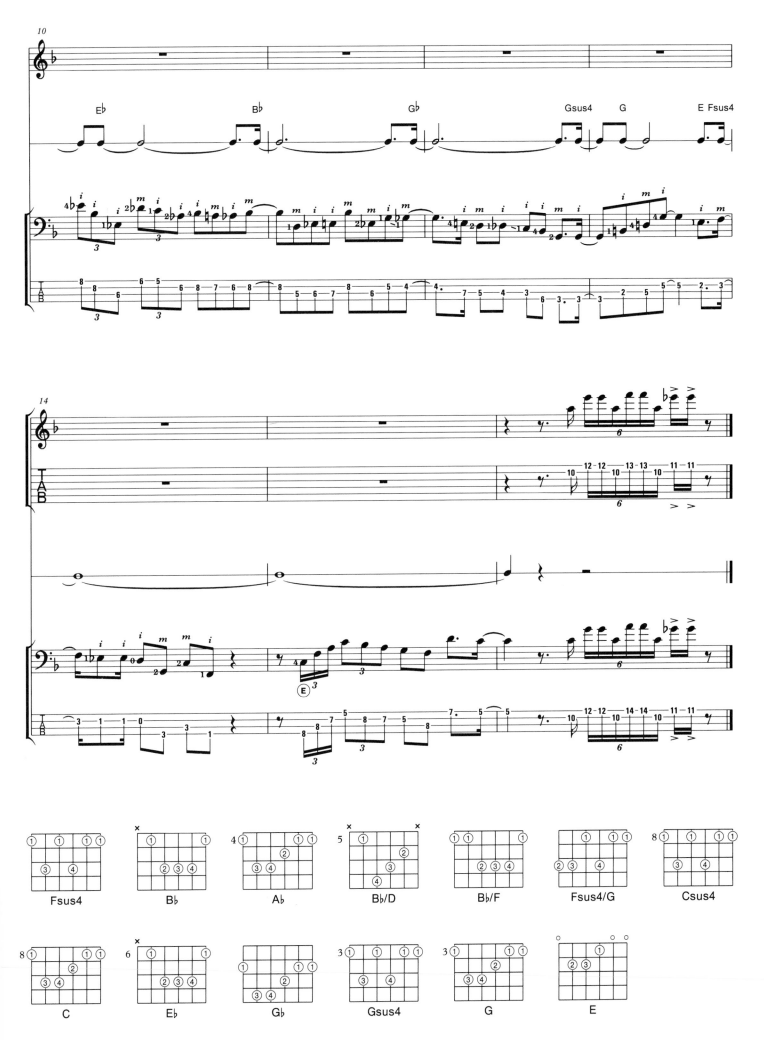

GENERAL INFORMATION

Open Strings

Bass Guitar

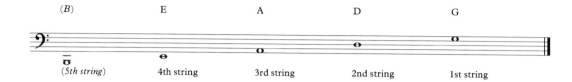

Rhythm/Lead Guitar

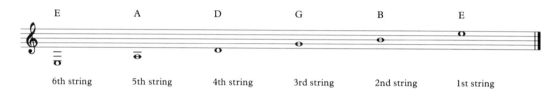

String Numbers

A number set in a circle indicates the string

- ① first string
- ⑥ sixth string

Position Numbers

A Roman numeral indicates the position of the left-hand fingers. The number shows the fret that is to be pressed by the first finger and assumes that the second, third and fourth fingers will 'look after' their respective frets above the position.

- II Second Position

  The first finger of the left hand is positioned at the second fret.

- V Fifth Position

  The first finger of the left hand is positioned at the fifth fret.

Bar and Half-Bar

For a bar, the first finger is laid flat across all of the strings. It is indicated by the letter C. For a half-bar, the first finger is laid flat across three or four strings. It is indicated by ½ C.

- CII Bar of the second fret
- ½CV Half-Bar of the fifth fret

Fingering

Left Hand

- 1 index finger
- 2 middle finger
- 3 ring finger
- 4 little finger

Right Hand

- p thumb
- i index finger
- m middle finger
- a ring finger

Slides

A slide is indicated by a short diagonal line and 'SL' (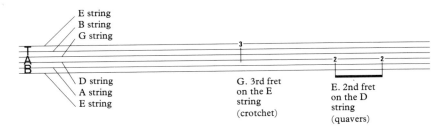). This should be distinguished from a 'finger-shift' which is shown by a diagonal line alone.

Tablature

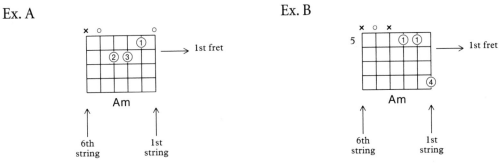

A number indicates which fret should be pressed. The line on which the number is placed shows the string. Rhythm is indicated by the note tails. (NB The four-string bass guitar uses only the lower four lines of tab.)

Chord Diagrams for Rhythm Guitar

(i)   The vertical lines represent the strings.
(ii) The horizontal lines represent the frets.
(iii) A circle with a number inside shows where a finger should be pressed, and which finger is to be used.
(iv) X indicates that a string is not to be played.
(v)   O indicates that a string is open.
(vi) Ex. A shows a chord in the first position. When a chord is played higher up the fingerboard, the number on the left of the box indicates the position. (Ex. B is in the 5th position).

The fingering and position of a chord is often based on the chords which precede and/or follow it. Although the chord shapes given at the end of each piece are the most suitable for that piece, occasionally a different chord position may be more convenient.

Note positions for bass guitar

Note positions for frets 1–4

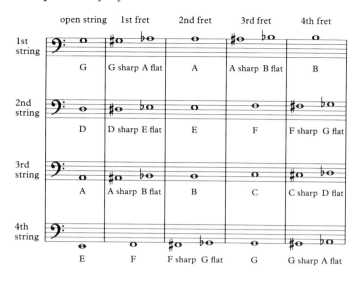

Note positions for frets 5–8

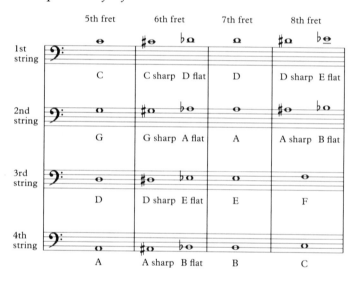

Note positions for frets 9–12

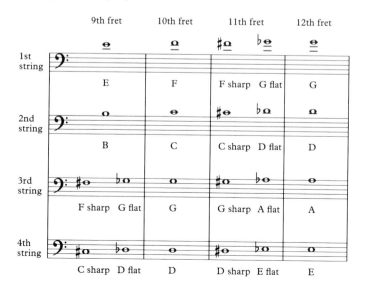

Note positions for the rhythm/lead guitar

Note positions for frets 1–4

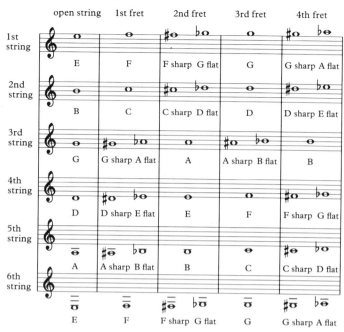

Note positions for frets 5–8

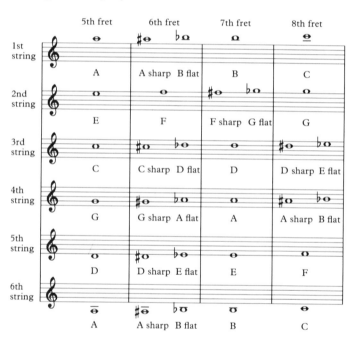

Note positions for frets 9–12